IN THE EMPIRE OF THE AIR

The Poems of Donald Britton

IN THE EMPIRE OF THE AIR

The Poems of Donald Britton

EDITED BY
REGINALD SHEPHERD AND PHILIP CLARK

NIGHTBOAT BOOKS
NEW YORK

Poems © 2016 by the Estate of Donald Britton
Preface © 2016 by Philip Clark
Introduction © 2016 by the Estate of Reginald Shepherd
Afterword © 2016 by Douglas Crase
All rights reserved
Printed in the United States

ISBN 978-1-937658-44-1

Design and typesetting by HR Hegnauer
Text set in Sabon

Cover painting: Copyright Estate of John Button, "Sunday Morning," 1980,
    Oil on canvas, Courtesy of ClampArt, New York City.

Interior photos:
Frontispiece: Donald Britton in Los Angeles, 1989. Used by courtesy of the
    Estate of Donald Britton.
Photo on page 90: Donald Britton and Douglas Crase in New York City, 1990, by
    Frank Polach. Douglas Crase and Frank Polach Papers. Beinecke Rare Book
    and Manuscript Library, Yale University. Used by courtesy of Frank Polach.

Cataloging-in-publication data is available from the Library of Congress

Distributed by University Press of New England
One Court Street
Lebanon, NH 03766
www.upne.com

Nightboat Books
New York
www.nightboat.org

CONTENTS

UNCOLLECTED AND UNPUBLISHED POEMS

ACKNOWLEDGMENTS

Reginald Shepherd's Acknowledgments
First and foremost, I would like to thank Donald Britton's literary executor, David Cobb Craig, for his help. Without his generous and enthusiastic response, this book would not have been possible. I would also like to thank Philip Clark, Dennis Cooper, Mark Doty, and Bernard Welt for their assistance in making this project much better than I could ever have made it on my own. I'm particularly grateful to Cooper and Welt for providing biographical information on Britton, about whom almost nothing has been written.

I'd like to thank Robert Philen for his love and support in this and every other endeavor.

Philip Clark's Acknowledgments
This book would not exist without Reginald Shepherd's vision and desire to bring Donald Britton's poetry back to public notice. I thank him for causing me to engage so intently with Donald's poetry, and I only hope that he would be pleased with the manuscript as it has been completed. Further thanks to Robert Philen, Reginald's partner and executor, for his encouragement to finish Reginald's work and permission to use the introduction that Reginald wrote for *In the Empire of the Air*.

Every writer would be lucky to have a literary executor as helpful as Donald's partner, David Cobb Craig, who has been unstintingly supportive at every stage of this book. His good cheer and hospitality are second-to-none. I'm proud, David, to have you as a friend.

In addition to writing a beautiful and necessary afterword, Douglas Crase scoured his memory and his papers for details, sharing with me Donald's letters to him. Doug's ideas made me think about Donald's poetry in new ways. He is a true gentleman, and his help has been crucial and valued.

Bernard Welt sent me photocopies of early poems, many of which are hard-to-find. He also allowed me to read Donald's letters to him, which are full of insight into Donald's personality. He is, as Donald said, "the Best of all Possible Bernards."

Both Larry Evans and Michael Faubion provided me with otherwise unknown poems, along with letters from Donald and ephemera from his time on the poetry scene. These materials gave a boost to the project at a critical time; thanks to each of them for their generosity to a complete stranger.

Stephen Motika and Nightboat Books have made great efforts on behalf of Donald's poetry and on behalf of the very idea of poetry's importance in an increasingly distracted world. Many thanks to Stephen for expressing early interest in the manuscript.

Numerous other individuals and institutions provided information, suggestions, contact information, or research assistance. Thanks to Kathleen DeLaney, Laine Farley, Amy Gerstler, Matthew Hittinger, Gary Kornblau, Gary Lenhart, Greg Masters, Richard Mathews, Edric Mesmer, Richard Reitsma, and Timothy Young; and to the librarians and other staff at Cornell University's Olin Library; the Library of Congress; New York University's Elmer Bobst Library, Rare Book and Manuscript Division; Poets House in New York City; the Poetry Collection at the University of Buffalo; and Yale University's Sterling Memorial Library.

PREFACE

by Philip Clark

To my regret, I never met Reginald Shepherd.

Reginald contacted me in July 2006, having heard from a fellow poet that I was working on editing the anthology that was to become *Persistent Voices: Poetry by Writers Lost to AIDS*. He wanted to make absolutely certain that I was going to include poems by Donald Britton, "a wonderfully gifted but under-published poet," and offered to send me a selection of Donald's work. Having first read and enjoyed some of Donald's poetry when I was in high school, I wouldn't have considered publishing the anthology *without* Britton's poetry, and Reginald was gratified—the way all of us are when we find another who is familiar with our obscurest enthusiasms—that someone else had read these strange and beautiful poems and shared his appreciation of them.

This note sparked a seven-month exchange of letters, as Reginald told me of his intention to compile a volume of Donald's selected poems and we both edited our respective books. We shared poems and information, but we also talked about our love for gay poetry anthologies like *The Son of the Male Muse*—where some of Donald Britton's poetry appeared—and traded tales of being openly gay teenagers at Southern governor's academies, he in Georgia and I in Virginia, almost twenty years apart. It was an easy, engaging correspondence, and it was heartening as well: each of us believing so intently, not only in our own work, but in the other's.

Sadly, Reginald passed away in 2008, not living to see *In the Empire of the Air: The Poems of Donald Britton* find a publisher. I do not know whether Reginald would agree with all the decisions I have made in completing the book, but I know he would be deeply pleased that Donald Britton's poems are available to a new sphere of readers prepared to appreciate their remarkable freshness of language and their highly particularized ways of experiencing the world.

As you once wrote to me: peace and poetry, Reginald.

INTRODUCTION

by Reginald Shepherd

I.

I first encountered Donald Britton's only published book, *Italy*, by happenstance in college. I was immediately taken by the poems' vivid yet subtle language and their wistful reticence, a sense of romance all the more powerfully affecting for its understatement. While clearly in the line of John Ashbery, Britton's poems have a greater intimacy even in their distances, and a verbal glamour the more enchanting for its modesty.

Britton's quiet but compelling voice stayed with me over the years, and it frequently occurred to me that I wanted to try to do something to bring his work to a larger audience. Work dies if it isn't read (though like Sleeping Beauty or Snow White it can be awakened by a reader's kiss), and I wanted to keep his work alive. *Italy* was published by poet and novelist Dennis Cooper's Little Caesar Press, small and long-defunct, and Britton never published another book. *Italy* received exactly two reviews, one in *The Village Voice* and one in *The Washington Review*. Britton is not listed in *Contemporary Authors*, nor is his work covered in any other reference work I know of, except for an article I wrote about him for editor Emmanuel S. Nelson's *Contemporary Gay American Poets and Playwrights*.

Thus this selected poems volume, which includes the complete texts of both *Italy* and his never-published second book, *In the Empire of the Air*, along with a substantial selection of uncollected and unpublished poems. I hope that it will serve to introduce this uniquely talented poet to a new generation of readers and writers.

II.

Donald Eugene Britton was born in San Angelo, Texas, in 1951, the son of Cyrus E. Britton and Vera Early Britton. He received his BA and his MA in American Literature (his 1976 MA thesis was on a performance approach to Shakespeare) from the University of Texas at Austin and his PhD in Literary Studies in 1979 from The American University, where he wrote his dissertation on Hart Crane's poetics of praise. On May 20, 1979, he moved to New York City and worked in direct mail fundraising and in advertising; in 1988 he moved from New York City to Los Angeles, where he worked as an executive at the advertising firm of Brierley and Partners. He died of AIDS on July 22, 1994.

While living in New York City Donald Britton was associated with what might be called the third generation of New York School poets, many of them gay, among them Joe Brainard, Dennis Cooper, Douglas Crase, Tim Dlugos, Kenward Elmslie, Brad Gooch, Steve Hamilton, and Bernard Welt. AIDS had a strong impact on this group: Brainard, Britton, and Dlugos died of the disease, and the survivors have long since gone their separate ways.

Britton was not a prolific poet, and writing did not come easily to him; a self-deprecating perfectionist, he invested a great deal of time and labor in each poem. His poems appeared in *Christopher Street*, *Epoch*, *The Paris Review*, and in several smaller journals. They also appeared in the anthologies *Coming Attractions: An Anthology of American Poets in Their Twenties*, *The Son of the Male Muse*, and *Ecstatic Occasions, Expedient Forms*. His one, rather brief book, *Italy*, was published in 1981 and featured blurbs from poets John Ashbery and Kenward Elmslie and novelist Edmund White. *In the Empire of the Air*, an even more brief volume than *Italy*, was to have been published by Little Caesar Press, but the project ran into financial difficulties. According to Cooper, Britton essentially stopped writing poetry in the late 1980s, though he frequently expressed a desire to write.

III.

The blurbs by Ashbery and White on the back cover of *Italy* accurately introduce the methods and themes of the work. Ashbery writes that "One is led gradually into these poems, which seem so quiet and open at first, like empty streets on the periphery of a city. Soon one realizes that for some time one has been involved in a strong dialectic with Donald Britton's remarkable and inspiring intelligence. By that time is too late to do anything but enjoy." Ashbery's comment emphasizes the effacement of self in Britton's poems; while there is often an "I," that pronoun sometimes serves as no more than a marker or a point of view, a place from which the poem sets out. As in T.S. Eliot's "The Love Song of J. Alfred Prufrock," or *The Waste Land*, the "you" that flickers in and out of the poems is at once and by turns the beloved, a friend, a companion wanderer, a doppelgänger or imago, and the reader. There is thus, despite the poems' lack of a fixed or defined self, the sense of intimacy I mentioned above, and an emotional openness all the more moving because of their surface reticence.

Many of Donald Britton's poems do not have "topics" in the conventional sense (though they do have places, indeed are places): they are not subject-centered in either meaning of the word. Britton doesn't usually write about himself or any version of himself, nor about characters or personae, but rather about states of mind as it moves through the world. His poems trace out the meanderings of embodied consciousness, teasing out the links between bodily experience and consciousness. The mind that these poems explore is particular and even individual, but it is not personalized in the post-Confessional manner, but abstracted and generalized, much as in the work of Ashbery himself, who is the single strongest influence on the work. As Britton writes in his poem "Sonnet" (which consists of fifteen unrhymed lines and is thus insistently askew formally, at once calling up and exorcising the ghost of the sonnet),

> My unkempt mind is yours, and the purity
> Of my body, and the lesions joining them.
> My outfit is yours, though you wear
> But one thing, amply clothed in the capsule
> Of a single sense of yourself.

Donald Britton's poems wear the outfit of self lightly, and rarely singularly; they explore not just what it might mean to be someone else, but what it might mean to be no one at all, or everyone. In them, as he writes in "Heart of Glass,"

> Personal history [is] annihilated, ground
> Into a very fine talc and gathered
>
> Into structures of air that are always
> Collapsing...
> But retaining [its] essential substance.

In his only statement on his work, the commentary on "Winter Garden" in the anthology *Ecstatic Occasions, Expedient Forms*, Britton writes that the formal rigor of the poem lies "in my attempt to 'non-personalize' or psychologically denature the poem—to detach it from any single speaker or communication context, yet maintain the illusion of a coherent, at times even elegant, discourse." Britton writes that "Winter Garden" has "no 'speaker,' no 'voice,' no 'persona,' no 'point of view.'" This is not true of all of his poems, but in all of them there is a distance from even the most personal and intense emotions, which are objectified rather than treated as an individual's possessions or characterizing features. This refusal to treat emotions as the property of any one self paradoxically makes them more available to the various selves who are the readers of the poem: as Britton writes in the poem entitled and on the question of "Inner Resources," "If you had them, they would take them. / So you give them away, freely."

Interestingly, there is more of a sense of a particular self in a particular place, a self rooted in childhood unhappiness and the imaginative escapes from that unhappiness, and also more grounding in specific spaces and locales, in Britton's uncollected work than in the poems of the two books that he assembled for publication. A poem like "My Mother's Afternoon Nap" is a fairly direct portrait of familial alienation, in which all the objects of the home bear the burden of that alienation. One wonders if he was less comfortable with a more direct representation of personhood or personality, if he felt that selfhood was something best dispersed or at least shared. This refusal to hold onto the self as a personal possession may be the source of the paradoxical intimacy of these seemingly impersonal poems. As he writes in "Impressionism" from *In the Empire of the Air*, which poem itself has a rather phenomenological title, "you // In this segment are several, / The difference between you eternal." No matter how close one seems to get, even to oneself, I is indeed always another.

In his blurb for *Italy*, Edmund White, one of Britton's mentors in New York City, writes that "The technique is dazzling, flowing from one tone of voice, formal and grave, and thence into something enigmatic and slangy. The sensation is like driving a car through an always changing but always beautiful landscape. Donald Britton has invented the tourism of the mind." White concludes that "This is a poet constructing poems in a more rigorously esthetic manner than almost anyone else in his generation." Indeed, their formal poise and elegance is one of the most striking features of Britton's poems.

Both Ashbery and White use the metaphor of a landscape or cityscape to describe Britton's poems, and this is quite apt, as the poems are (again, like Ashbery's) often about what might be called the experience of experience. They are wordscapes through which the reader journeys, marveling at their various features, some shining, some rather understated, but glistening when glimpsed more closely: as he writes in "We Loved the Inexact,"

> Several other things called
> Attention to themselves
> In the act of crawling quietly
> Out of view toward an out there
> Not located on any map.

Landscape, physical and psychic, is central to Britton's work, and it is these mapless locations that his poems sketch out for the receptive reader.

In this regard Britton is a follower not only of John Ashbery but of the French Symbolist poets, especially Mallarmé, who sought a pure poetry, what could be called a poetry in, of, and for itself. As Britton writes in *Ecstatic Occasions, Expedient Forms*, his poems are a way "to project oneself toward that point where one's words cease to comment on *any* experience, but become an experience in and of themselves: empty of discursive content, perhaps [though replete with what Susanne Langer calls virtual speech and symbolic form], but full of all manner of things *language* wants to say, but people usually don't." Britton's work explores the "White Space"

> Beginning where words drop off
> In a remnant of music too simple
> For speech.

Reginald Shepherd's Note on the Text

Many of Donald Britton's uncollected and unpublished poems exist in several versions, usually with no indication of which he considered to be the final text. In such cases, I have selected what seemed to me to be the best readings. I have also silently corrected grammatical and spelling errors.

The poems "The Sky Is Clear, But It's Raining" and "Extensive Landscape Beyond" are in some ways versions of one another, but they seemed sufficiently distinct to warrant publication as separate poems. The poem "The Good Hour" shares some phrasing with each of these, but otherwise seems even more distinct.

Philip Clark's Note on the Text

Reginald's conception for this book omitted four poems from *Italy*: the title poem, "Elevators I," "Elevators II," and "*Non Piangere, Donald!*" I have reinstated them so that readers may experience the whole of Donald Britton's only published book. Additionally, some of Donald's uncollected poems did not come to light until after Reginald passed away. Of those poems, I have selected "An Amorous Day," "Serenade," "Signs," and "Here and Now." Readers may judge whether those inclusions were warranted.

Reginald's original manuscript suggests that he did not see published versions of many of the poems outside of *Italy*. When published versions exist, I have generally given preference to them.

UNCOLLECTED AND
UNPUBLISHED POEMS

LARGE WINTER SCENE

Hendrick Avercamp
1585-1634, a deaf-mute

Birds cling to
the starkest
wind-scorched branch
and shudder frost
from their
wings. The people
skate on a
frozen lake where
the ice-
boat is moored
at the willow
stump and the
sleigh-horse's
blue plume rancors
the conical
ladies. I may
dream of shouldering
sticks and walking
in horse-dung
over the frozen
lake to the
rim of the world.

AN AMOROUS DAY

An amorous day and not to be denied;
toothpaste coffee toast portend
the cold sea-swell of my urges.

Aromatic whisker parted,
raw and swollen tentacle tamed, incognito—
and every pustule in its place.

Morning scud retreats; the tennis court
and leafy pool unobscured
by winter's diminished eloquence.

Novelist N and Poet P describe the scene:
an arcane underlip skims the post-tumescent beads
and bedsheets will be washed and flap dry in the sun.

HART CRANE SAVED FROM DROWNING
(ISLE OF PINES, 1926)

He stood a long time while the USS *Milwaukee*
oxidized at the salt-wash pier. The succulent
hot stiletto beach pitched his nerves like waves
and waves bombed thunder cloud to palm.

A dolphin materialized drilling
through serrated foam. Bacardi and fifteen-cent
Corona-Coronas slaked his thirst for sailors
now: he puked in volleys on ignited sand.

Fish-eye, coruscated scales of surf, the bird
with a note Rimbaud speaks of as 'making you blush'—
coral negatives plashed gold and azure plaster
in the harbor: death could come like a blackout drunk.

But the naked Cubano all testicles and rod
laving amid ripe tendrils of the water ridges
trumped fate with desire; so he postponed his resolve
for six years and a boat and a woman.

ALL SAINTS' EVE

for Terry Galloway

We play anxiety
like a game:
nobody told us
as spoon-size squirrels
to save our nuts.

Still, you have prepared
your winter home—
galoshes, shawl, and umbrella
near the door
for emergencies
when ice scavenges 25th Street
or fog rolls in
like a trashcan
soundless
at your feet—
now that the town
is the color
of a fortune in pennies.

• • •

O Great Poker Face!
Allow us always
a flabby chair and a rocker.
Renew the coffee bean
each season
in the mountain rain forest.
Endeavor to protect
the lemons
in our lemonade
from the worms that kill.

O One!
Instruct our nervous eyes
to seek out love
in the quarter peep-show
in the alcoholic mask
in the monotony
of good weather
and in all rooms
where expecting least
we desire it most.

MY MOTHER'S AFTERNOON NAP

The table, lamp, and chair
strain against the ordinary light
that props up the window
spilling needles on the carpet,
shade recomposing on the sill.

Mother wraps her fear into a towel
and shrinks upon her bed,
denying to the potent afternoon
the touch of quick emotions.
The engines of the house are still.

The stillness is a bullet in her brain.
Upon the stake the ivy curls
like infant Jesus bloody on the grass.
The countertops are polished bright
and blue-veined as the mirrors.

Clouds stroke the sky into autumn
while Mother sleeps and hates
the life that hurt her into sleep—
bound to one so much not herself,
she his body's inarticulate host.

She feels the pillow crease her cheek,
uncertain in the ache of waking.
No gloss of love dispels
the image of those angels she attends,
bow-tied detectives who take her away.

THE GOOD HOUR

A blank tape is the record
Of our gracious sustained attention
To the sound of the probabilities

Of sound. When such music plays
We are analyzed
Into hundreds of accordion-like units,

Each a box from which
In spiky silhouette a backlit figure
Seems to wave. And the moment

Is held together
By pressure, so the densely punctuated
Phrases may be heard, the scenery

Squeezed from bright
Articulate tubes.

ANATOMY

Today's meditation is translated from the French.
In certain passages, a trace of the original's clarity
Survives, but as a skinless body
Now standing before the gates of a Medieval town!

Is it poised to instruct us in how to draw
New lines of inquiry from the studied irresolution
Of its own figure, or to answer still another question…
Not the one we asked?

Slowly the light seeps from lamp to page.
Who would not relish the luxury, just for an hour,
Not to be falling promiscuously over everyone everywhere
In all dimensions, at incredible speed?

This body has not moved for centuries.

VALENTINE

for David Cobb Craig

At first, we had ways of talking
That filled up the evening
Until some things could be said. It was a made-up
Situation in which lives could be lost.
Whatever that was now grows inside
Our bodies—a spongy, pulpy cell—
Causing pieces of paper we hold
In our hands to appear

And disappear. All I ask
Is to take me away from this place,
To another place, very much like
This place, where we can meet
And six months later
Be married. You laughed and went with me.

THE SKY IS CLEAR, BUT IT'S RAINING

Under the trees, where everything
Is still possible in prescribed doses:
Hundreds of accordion-like units
Without edges. But there is no unwinding

Of minutes to stay the execution
Of a rain-shot weekend in early
Beach weather, no elixir
To revive the amputated flower

Still kicking on its ghost-stem
In a bowl of water, no direction
In which to steer
The hapless, puzzled out-of-towner

Other than straight ahead,
To the sheer drop-off
Where his guidebook gutters
Or deposits him, addressless,

In thin air.

EXTENSIVE LANDSCAPE BEYOND

Having gazed too long
Through the windows of a car or train
At woozy scenery squeezed
From bright, articulate tubes,

Though standing still, our motion
Has not ceased to move,
Filling empty spaces
That don't exist until the rush

Of lateral perspectives
Makes them visible, accessible
To sight only when the light
Disclosing them's annulled. See—

The bay, some clouds, a hill
Where suddenly pertinent trees
Now loom. And so many people
Tugging at the edge

Of the sidewalk, living
In response to an unfavorable
Editorial. How long
Before their guidebooks gutter,

Depositing them all, addressless,
In thin air?

THE BUILDINGS

The buildings are there now,
convincingly: a shape, an attitude
we get undressed for, nearer
night's astonished irregularities.
You can see them, as by coincidence
we came to see each other, recanting
certain portions of darkness
unmentioned in the foaming stars.

We entered the buildings: the multiplicity of possible buildings
narrowed to these buildings. Yet even among this limited range
of buildings thousands of choices remained to be made, are being
made, for the order of the buildings is the very condition of their
complexity and hence the cause of our confusion in them.

At night we drove past the buildings, less interested in the buildings
themselves than in our remarks about them. The buildings were
studded with light. Taken as a whole the buildings comprised a
system of lights, in the blackened interstices of which was a secret to
be yielded up to remind us of something.

The buildings assert a meaning
more than any particular laughter
at them, being absent from that part
of the sky gathering their outline.
We lift them in our sleep high
above the possibility of continuing
to live in this slightly ruined state,
pulled upward by gravity toward
the disaster that will prove conclusive
this time amid the extinguished suns.

UNATTACHED

The raw kitchen light
was a substitute for something
else, the rain an activity
going on and pleased to be left
alone, unspoken of. I have
developed, then, this
leaping-back motion as a device
for getting out of the way
of these next few things as
they happen: a telephone
ringing in the desert, scrawny
winter sparrows like half-
notes on the fire escape
outside my window, the movements
of the President to and fro
on the carpet of the Oval Office.

An eager wanting to call you
by your peculiar name, peeling
off the residue silence,
discretion, and distance leave
on everything. These days
have a way of knowing what we want
and putting it in the closet
and swallowing the key, as if
the risks taken simply expanded
our opportunities for being
rejected. How many "Ah-ha!"
responses, after all, can any of us
endure in the course of a season?

Bite after miserable bite
and still no fluffy center to this
candy bar, as though consuming it
were the perfect demonstration
of its suave emptiness.

My desire is like coral, growing
up out of the disintegration
of other things, a shape
into which masses of watery
light are poured. My love
exists to prove you impossible.

"My brains are falling out.
You could pick them up,
but you are sitting on my chest
waiting for the water to boil.
Kiss me. Assume I have
something you want and take it
from me. Evening is cresting
into a desperate darkness
arguing against my insufficient
identity. I am boring you.
I don't remember what I just said."

THE PHOTOGRAPH

Everyone is in a jeep
Pushing sideways to the past.
Their squinting postulates a sun
And more sperm than usual,
Which is their way of saying "Thank you"
To the jeep, now sunk in a crevice.

But how the jeep soars through the corn field!
The wind starches their eyelids.
A firefly civilization establishes itself.
The war grows near, now far away,
The horse apples within reach.
They invent the war as they go along.

And the jeep? An obstacle to itself,
It curves through the expanding grain.

TALKING TO MYSELF

I have pondered
the teacup

the solemn
saucer

the sugar
and cream;

I know
upstairs

someone I don't know
ponders a voice

and someone
in another room

cracks perilous ice
pours a pony of gin—

to make
a carnival

to affirm
a principle

of motion
of going on and on;

I have pondered
the chair

you sit in
the table

you write at
the letters

I wrote
and you read

ZONA TEMPERATA

I may see on my wall
a street of Paris, by Utrillo,
where black figures walk,
as I walk, in the evenings
past houses walled by white stone;
each house has a
garden and trellis and
shuttered windows. On the wall
in my room is
a suburban street of Paris,
painted by Utrillo,
le vierge, le vivace, et le bel aujourd'hui.

The work of Utrillo
        presents the common streets: rooftops
          and doorways and pavement.
           There are sometimes trees.
          One can imagine life on those streets
          as their residents know it,
here on the wall of my room.
          In the street below my window
the gutters are clogged by leaves
and grass and branches
clipped by the wind. The glass of my
window is thin.

        A street of Paris, done by Utrillo,
        hangs on the wall in my room.

A REAL LIFE

I awaken—
a clam between
cool sheets.

A nude bather
like Cézanne's.

And showering
in the dark
I imagine
my body.

POEM

Scrupulous, I left
at dawn: a violent
mind that contained
itself like a seed.

Having prepared the
phrases and left them
unspoken. Now rain's
black-and-white film

threads dry air and
mercenary thunder.

NANCY TO SLUGGO

"Why are you always
late?
To thus disfigure time
bespeaks
a thinness of character.
Your bristled
dome
now fails to amuse, to arouse
as in the past
I remarked
it did.

I myself
am keen
on the lunar prospect
perpetually
before my gaze.
Its order
satisfies
my natural thrall for form
which you
I take it
mock.

Love must assume its place
amid
the total arrangement
of things.
I have tried, dear, to adore
the fringeless clouds

your thoughts.
Pay no heed to the goldfish
near the window
they are
dead."

'EXPECTING B FROM 4 TO 4:30'

Something in the air
I would call its tone
and the tea things
gently washed upon the table:

the afternoon
so pleasingly corresponds
to my notations in this book.

Ah, the paintings
drink up all the light
I think I'm getting
an erection—

the image of B
emerging through the image
of the door. Imagine!

"Even the dust is in its place,"
where could I have heard that?
My room is composed
of the sum of its qualities:

its patches of color
itching inside the eye
and the quilling of these motes.

The lives of others, too,
are strange. B exists
as a function of his unhappiness;
he has often uttered this.

And through the years
his words have ceased to serve him.
One never knows what to say to B.

FORSAKEN HEART

I am clean as a monument.
Moment to moment I await
the telephone, the knock,
the functionary with the check
and fresh chromosomes: a new life.

I have been sitting here a long time,
wormy as Hieronymus,
contemplating a revised persona...
inevitably I turn Verlaine,
all soapy and domestic—

coeur délaissé but not *supplicié*—
young Arthur on the chaise,
Sebastian tracks beneath his sleeve,
puffing an immortal shag
and later a hero to queers.

"OF THE PERMANENT SECRET CRISIS..."

Of the permanent secret crisis
Little is known
Except the details. White fiery blossoms
Burn themselves out,

Ten thousand bicycles pursue
Their messengers, but the living goes on
In another quarter,
Setting forth each day toward a still point

Fixed on the horizon,
As toward some miracle after which
The cripple must push his own wheelchair
Home.

MENTAL NOTE

Must get down to business ASAP.
The morning air's thickly seeded
With importunings, wedged between
White and black spaces of the crossword grid

Gradually taking shape in the monitor.
Nothing needs to be said, but is somehow
Communicated, in the time that gets pulled
From a hat or grows, like an air fern,

Out of nothing.

SERENADE

for Seema Kirmani

You know me as the lighthousekeeper
Knows the weather, at night, on all sides.
Sometimes the summer sky is a hollow, dark
Socket and I feel as empty as my clothes
When I'm not in them. To feel fresh,
Like blood from a cut, is best, and to look
Up at the stars coming out, like tears
Coming out of a face, is also best.
Thus each of our gestures amounts
To a critique of the whole concept of action.
Not one of the spasms of sunlight
Splayed across the bed is undeserving
Of my attention. We are attached,
Painfully, to the individual histories
Of these things, which count on us,
Like children, to do right by them.

I should like to become better acquainted
With the facts of your biography, even
The uninteresting chapters where you just
Lie around all day, smoking cigarettes
And thumbing through magazines. The others,
Those in which love or lack of love
Coils your sympathies to a point of flame,
Like sun through a magnifying glass,
Consume themselves in their own intensity
And seem never to have happened.
Humans cannot bear too much unreality:

The interlude of splendor, when everything
Was on the verge of falling into place
And yielding up, at last, its superabundance
Of pleasure undiluted by pain or pain
From which no particle of pleasure was absent,
Must and should give way to afternoons
Like these, washed out as an old signature,
The negative of dazzling. The voluptuousness
Of the act is in the waiting and the not knowing
And the wanting and yet not wanting to know
The outcome and the hope that the outcome
This time will be that there will be no outcome
But that time will accommodate itself
To a kind of infinite delay in which
You are moving forward and not standing still,
Yet never approaching or catching sight of,
Through waves of distance, whatever's there.
If our dreams are unattainable, that is all
The more reason to keep on dreaming,
As there can be no question of the fully achieved
Life or the flawless consummation of anything.

And there can be no doubt that the only
Immortality is in not dying and not in what
I write or do, though I wish you could be there
Forever, listening and accepting, as though
None of it were really silly or wrongheaded,
But somehow beautiful, like the story I heard
Once of someone drifting out of a safe harbor,
Stunned by a million lights, on the Star Ferry.

NOVEMBER

for Bernard Welt

Tonight you are privy
To the stars' most intimate
Thoughts about you. Under
Their menace, edges of furniture
Seem like old news
As tears fall single file.

Leaves drift in and out
And the leaf-baskets ache
To catch them, the last tile
Of sky placed definitively
Above this useless decay,
The moon a white spool.

Your heart is casual. There are wings you will never know. You are
putting on your goofy smile again, which means you are in love,
whose colors are indistinguishable from lust and infinite vigilance.

The manic gloom
Has fled your apartment.
A talc of moonlight dusts
Your lemons with surmise,
Like a new surfeit,
To tell us about it.

NOTES ON THE ARTICULATION OF TIME

It becomes a critical account
of all that's spoken, done:
the drawing in of breaths, even,
these nights whose atmosphere
reminds us of mountains,
white volumes of air. We need

these narratives, we want them:
the city lies before us
and some one person in the sleeve
of a streetlamp awaits
our enraptured attention
as we await the concept of the city

which tells us how we move
in the particolored geographies
about us. We can't be certain
we are moving toward this person
nor do we require certitude.
It is enough to acknowledge

the movement itself, shavings
of light inscribing a circle.
Our childlike sense of the other
bears these forces toward
completion and renewal,
a lexis of infatuated sounds.

SIGNS

A landscape blunders toward the room.
Rain pours. Snow falls. The city
Wears a white uniform as night
"Comes on," seductive, like valium.

I have this feeling, which sleds off
Into the street. It concerns you,
Somehow. My unintended meaning is
"You image in it the sadness and pity
You experience as a permanent state
Though realized through different objects."
This is known as "projection,"
As when, tilting the visor of the lamp
Toward the victim with the wine glass,
This is known as "the third degree,"
An eagle's shadow thrown upon the wall
By a clever manipulation of the hands.

The feeling returns, "somewhat dazed,
But, thank the good Lord, unharmed."
Soon it will be "as good as new"
And resume "a normal, productive life,"
Albeit a limited and unhappy one.
The possibility of other feelings,
Equal in intensity, is suggested
Though not predicted. This is explained
By "anal retentiveness," the unhealthy urge
To shield one's anus from others.
The room will then become emptied of light,
Blackened by the pretense of hands as wings.

The snow drifts apologetically down
And "re-enacts the old, despairing scene."
Its moral is that we want the same "things,"
We just have different names for them.
This is known as "desire," in which "fear"
Is present, like a guest with a gun,
If you interpret "guest" as a reference
To you and the threat you represent.
But the guest grows old and "passes away"
The way a minor chord yields to the air,
His teeth dropping like ice on pink taffeta
As the absence of light is the eagle's shape.

HERE AND NOW

The start of the new era
Of desperation is starting over.

Meanwhile you and your bronze friend
Run naked through the yellowed broom sage,
Suspended vaporously above life
Like high pressure systems. A redolent
Cascade of voices from the lawn
As the next new hope something will happen
Ascends the orangerie steps, an endless
Unpunctuated sentence that seems at the time
To illuminate everything, as if a giant
Had stepped between you and the sun,
Sucking the light and punching a hole
In space, revealing infinite vistas
Of anticipation and delay.

These things have no beginning, or rather
Were set in motion long before we became
Their facsimile, thinking ourselves privileged
To secret information, not sensible
Of how the world contrives with enormous
Duplication of labor to rid itself of us
And perform its little routines
Solo in the galactic swimming pool
That is at last a total stage. It is
The amusing notion life might someday
Not be confusing that coordinates
Our award-winning sentiments these last days
Of summer, preparatory to the paint-by-number

Rush of autumn, the colors balking
Within their lines, which as a kid
Was the hardest part and apparently still is.
You must do something, though, not caring
What it is, so long as, when the day ends,
You're able to claim that this thing
Has been accomplished, brought nearer
The perfection toward which it ludicrously
Aspires, then put aside to be resumed
At a point just over the next rise yonder
Where suddenly pertinent trees now loom.

ITALY

WHITE SPACE

Beginning where words drop off
In a remnant of music too simple
For speech. I walked back and forth
Across the park as between two worlds,
Neither of them mine, like one
Emerging from one dream into another
Dream, and so on and so forth;
Autumn arriving with heavy breathing
And giant billboard apples
And a kind of built-in auspiciousness
Threshing the air like applause.

The austerity of the setting
And the mind's horniness might produce
A fresh coordination of the accents,
As though a behind-the-scenes
Explanation of their workings were
Possible if not forthcoming. Horns,
Timbrels, harmonicas, flexatones:
These could contribute to the din
Even now loosening robes of silence
Over Mouseville, pouring into a pause
Endlessly prolonging itself

Out of the time that used to be
Left over for the give-and-take
Of ordinary life, mowing the lawn,
Polishing brass, etc. Now "earth
Blankets herself with the sea
After mating with the sky and the sons

Of earth penetrate the mother in death."
From this, a museum must rise,
Flawless and inevitable as the snow
That chills the feet of walking statues:
Receive a horrible birth.

FOUR POEMS

1. *Variety Lights*

Above and beyond this aimlessness
Light in fistfuls
Scores the upside-down window on a blond floor
The skywriting's reflected backwards in
And red buildings lop off the sky
Somewhere down near where the canal starts
Ringing like glass
To be near the flower you think is dead.
Negotiating startled air
The children had lodged in their stomachs
The cow getting rained on on TV
Discovers our eyes starving for weather
Reconsidering again
The auxiliary entertainment
The skywriting could have been used for
If they were lighting the stadium up.

2. *Inner Resources*

If you had them, they would take them.
So you give them away, freely,
Like coupons in the newspaper.
But some of them come back
Changed, as in a cloud
Each boy or girl names a different figure:
Examples. Or one idea, expressed
A million times, might seem a million ideas

Modified by a single factor.
So are these fireworks
Ingots of flame crusted on the sky
The viewer causes to glow in his room
When the light darkens
And morning binds him to some new word
Far from the room and men's efficiency?

3. *History*

Each gesture "speaks," light pressing like a scarf
Across the throat whose breath
Sinks into a well of air, surrogate
For all that energy gently dissipating
In anticipation of all that stays. Not the torpor
That fixes everything in the immobility of ruins,
But a life of incident
Duly reported in the newspapers,
Full of domestic terror and the thrill
Of passing to and fro over memorized routes
Which stick to the mind like music,
Scrutinizing the use we make of them
Season by season. This geography we learn
First as a name, first as a body.

4. *Sonnet*

My unkempt mind is yours, and the purity
Of my body, and the lesions joining them.
My outfit is yours, though you wear
But one thing, amply clothed in the capsule

Of a single sense of yourself. You tire
Of our games. I never tire
Of them or you or the feelings that correspond
To our being together in this neutral climate.
Our natures are cold but for love
Dreadfully radiant in us. Emptiness abounds.

The conch bears no sea sounds, only the silence
Of a wave's interior calm. I think of you
And light breaks over still water. Already
You are forgetting this: the day, the hour,
The primary colors.

CAPITAL LIFE

Too much like one who bears a resemblance
But is not who he is taken for,
As in dreams the ideal is written in every line.
Or as one roaming hither and thither

Across the surface of the earth seeking
Perfect and autonomous quiet in which
To pronounce those syllables he knows: that
There are endless styles but only one subject

And this is it. Yet blankness still invades
The side of a wall, nailing you hypnotically
To a single course of action
Whose consequences spangle prematurely

Like morning vapors washing their burden
Of light through bamboo shades. Perhaps.
But does the ability to count presuppose
Some grander, intuitive understanding

Of mathematics, or does one just get by
With plain addition and subtraction
And the *sang-froid* of one's convictions?
Or are these numbers like signs from God,

Clear yet inexplicable, denoting the in-between
States of being and aspiring to the condition
Of a bookmark, dividing the known
From the unknown, neutral with respect to each?

When the time has come to speak, with what
Excuse will we deny ourselves the opportunity,
Choosing silence rather than an inferior
Blessedness, as if we might never grow up,

But extend the prologue so long that it becomes
The tale itself, as so much cautious preparation
Leading to a description of breathlessness,
White porticoes? A kind of endlesslessness.

WE LOVED THE INEXACT

We loved the inexact
Replicas in the museum: our life
Had no human scale, but tore
Apart little by little
As by a mysterious flowering
Light is torn from the river.

Thinking that way, we moved
Along, slightly paranoid, through
Husks the afternoon became.
The new construction site
Was seen to be a point
Grappling the emergent line.

Several other things called
Attention to themselves
In the act of crawling quietly
Out of view toward an out there
Not located on any map,
Not my map at any rate.

An upward motion swept everything
Up, way up, into a stratosphere
Of positive sexual charges
And then a downward motion swept
Everything down again and before
Became a different version.

We were pleased that the place
Thus prepared us to accept
The blank stares these moments
Offered, tossing us aside
Into packing crate or closet
To list the misremembered items.

Still uneasy, though, these things
Irradiating pleasure as we lost
Them, the concept of the mud nymph
Sufficient to explain
This mud but unable to tell us
What to do about it.

We loved the jostling
Forward, the sensation
Of flight seen as gesture,
Eclipsing much pain
As the pain of separation
Is eclipsed by a dream of union.

Otherwise, a slow progress
Toward several trees there
In a distance, growing larger
And older and clearer and
Finer as we approach the option
Of turning, finally, away.

SEPTEMBER NIGHT

for Seema Kirmani

Nothing told us it would work out
This way, that nothing
Stays put in the drawer of itself.

Down by the watering can
A squirrel is belief, whatever
He is thinking. And again, and at

The water's edge, and for a long time
After summer vacation
Pieces of the wreck stabbed the shore
Whose revenue of loss engorged
The ribboned cone of a shell
And played the ear its thousand phrases.

But the foreseeable future ended
And we are falling backwards
Into the view from here that is too bashful
To be looked at or taken from a pocket
Ingenious as the heart's restive
Knowledge of the back of your head.
Where were we when a slab of morning
Overturned the previous day's verdict
Now placed in evidence against us?

I'm still thinking, the kite that that
Vertebra of clouds is the tail of,
Lifting me up like a number

Carried to the top of a column of figures
Sheerly by the logic of it
As a last-gasp oompah note drains
The afternoon of resourcefulness
And fear. The cloned minutes pass,
Each resembling the original
In everything except
Not having been predicated on prior
Misgivings, merely beguiled
Out of the need of space to put
Some distance between it
And the people who remained behind
After departing. Theirs is the sum
To be added up, once the
Indecipherable messages delivered today
Become the sign of how much
Waits to be said, in buildings
That are torn down and built again
And condemned, then raised by night.
And every flaw is equalized.

HEART OF GLASS

Every act expresses a wish, surviving
A lot of living and shifting
Into new forms of a sad decorum
Like a science uncommitted to the facts:

Squinting into the sun like one
Getting old very fast, the past something
Made of bricks laid end to end
To the top of yon hill of waves

And sinking, thinking still of you
For whom no wave grieves, no radio
Goes dead, but mentioned in the
Acknowledgments for various kindnesses.

Then, awakening, the day is perhaps
Too young to hurt you, still adulterated
With remembered pain and hope
Whose emblem is the paradisiacal slope

Of light on the Poster Child's
Limp, empty sleeve. Either that,
Or the beautiful seed at the heart
Of an apple, which promises that this

Corny emotionalism can go on
Indefinitely, sluicing into the shape
Of its own ingenuity as light pours
Into its speed, the bubble you are

Floating in reducing all that floor plan
To wasted space, the gaudy interior
Of a Venetian bead painted to resemble
Someone's idea of how time would look

If the distances between things could be
Squeezed into a corner to make room
For what it takes from us, leaving behind
Instructions for reproducing the diorama

Exactly as it happened, in the same way
To each of them, so that in the end
Personal history was annihilated, ground
Into a very fine talc and gathered

Into structures of air that are always
Collapsing. Such was the benign, giddy
Environment in which Freddy found himself,
Though as yet somewhat queasy about

What the Fire-God had told him, feeling
Not unlike the disgorged meal of a panther,
Chewed by something black and terrible
But retaining his essential substance,

Putting all the rest behind him
Like a buried parent, to become the hero who,
Elated at the portrayal of things beyond his ken,
Shouldered his people's glorious future.

SPONTANEOUS BRUISES

Another kind is different in these trees
From its urban self, a joke preserved.
But the fragments become natural marvels
Or new species, holding up always
The idea of the gemlike core.

The old days in the unthreatened home are beautiful.

And the figure seems more real to him
Because of the explanations written on him,
The mind pursuing its dream of coherence
On and on in diminishing congruent boxes

Slowly saluting the four points of the sky
And kneeling on the ground amidst azure powder
Sprinkled with golden stars in imitation
Of the firmament. How lightly they spin,
Borne up by the impalpable ether polishing itself
Around you, waxing and waning as cats' eyes
And panthers' spots expand and shrink:
You run in the blue of your sky and I
Stay motionless upon earth like a solid block
Or lozenge of sculptural uselessness.

This space, now occupied, is the most comfortable
Imaginable. We have gone far up inside
And found a hidden den, private room after
Private room, a realm of studies all prepared,
Granting perfect seclusion by being broken
Into indistinguishable increments where a path
Is untraceable and pursuers get lost, all at once.

XEROGRAPHY

Black dots adding up, snow on the parking lot, footsteps of the
parking lot attendant, coins slipping through the parking lot
attendant's fingers as he crosses the parking lot toward a motorist,
the motorist's gloved hand holding a famous city newspaper, a
photograph on an inside page showing snow drifts and black
and gray cars bunkered in snow before a famous monument, the
monument flaring up into the rock salt sky from which snow is
falling on the baseball cap of the parking lot attendant, waves of
white monotony whooshing past the face of a pedestrian entering
a black office tower, fluorescent light tubes buzzing as he rises
to the eleventh floor, steps from the elevator to the window, the
white, vague city below, taut as fresh sheets, the businessman in
his business suit standing at the window, turning from papers at
his desk on which words are typed analyzing the economy of a tiny
developing African nation, where noon sun blanches a plain of tall
grass as herdsmen scan the plain for the leopard that struck a calf,
tugged it to the ground by the neck and clenched the neck tightly in
its jaws until, bleating blood, the calf was dead, a nearby camera
crew from an important television network filming the entire
incident from a copse of baobob trees, the khaki safari shirt of the
head cameraman attractively unbuttoned to the waist revealing a
hard flat stomach flossed with blonde hairs, the spoor of a pack of
migrating wild dogs thick with flies next to the head cameraman's
right boot, the dog pack coursing miles away along a dry river bed
scorched into a billion deviations from the spring.

NON PIANGERE, DONALD!

1.

Weird wind at the window.
Inside-of-pocket sky, close, empty,
cool, cigarette-wrapperish
and shadowless.

No preliminary smells of ho-hum rain.
Wind still acting up.
Looking out, a fat Ann Miller,
a dog on the next roof,

woman following man following man
following man, hair all messed up.
Darkening sky. Papers scuttling.
Baby Tarzan yell from schoolyard

full of Babies and Tarzans.

2.

The tedium of wanting you.
An Emotionally Intense Moment.
I make one two three four
slash marks like a prisoner

counting the times I've stood
before the mirror wondering
what you'd think seeing me
crying like this because of you.

Little forests of five trees,
one of which is falling THUMP
across the others. I'm not
there and you're not there

but I hear it.

3.

The meaning of Being is the question
to be formulated. The steak
and the salad and the baked potato
were delicious.

Breeze up. Airplanes gurgling
out into the silent Atlantic, tracing
me-to-you parabolas: semicolon
quarter moon and evening star

and streetlamp making two shadows
behind me and in front of me.
Me following me following me.
In the middle of the street I remember

that time I cracked my head open.

ELEVATORS I

An enormous list:
coming and goings, nights and mornings,
births and deaths
and rebirths and second deaths
and little lapses like grace notes
where sadness surges in:

sadness surges in,
a passing-windshield light-effect
on the ceiling.
Would you prefer it some other way?
I'm versatile.
I'm hungry.
I'm hot.
I'm not really sad either.
I'm happy, it's just that this happiness
isn't the happiness I expected or sought
and for a time I confused
this happiness with the sadness
I thought I was experiencing.
I feel a lot better now.

Oooh. That should give you
an indication of the improvement.
Oooh, there it goes again.
And again,
only I didn't say 'Oooh' this time.
I can't explain it,
but it feels terrific,
like a totally fulfilled infatuation
or a California Lifestyle apartment ad.

ELEVATORS II

You are leaving
and I am low,
lower than the low notes on a cello,
lower than the stock exchange,
lower than Elizabeth Taylor's chronic
lower back pain.

We Mohawk, however, are a sturdy people.
Here on the high girders, can you believe it,
we don't look down. All we do is dance, in fact:
samba and rumba and cha-cha. The foreman
brings up whores and we fuck them
standing on our hands and whistling
while the others dance and make smoke signals.
It's great: we love them through the pores
because we do everything that way,
to all appearances like eagles mating in air.

We Swiss are a fastidious people,
attentive to such things as fingernails.
Our manicures are exquisite: the little moons
have four phases like the real moon
and we always know what day it is, what time
it is, and how everybody is feeling.
Lately we've had a thing for the Mohawk.
We admire their extraordinary balance
and timing sense. Hourly we look up, hoping
to see on the graph of the unfinished towers
YOU ARE CORDIALLY INVITED TO THE REST OF MY LIFE

in furious passionate smoke.

LA PLUS BELLE PLAGE

Clever clouds unfurling new stratagems,
Going at it like bantams:
Coiled, calm, coiled again, recoiled.
Ingenious assortment of clouds
And arrangements of the assortment.
With each new assortment
A new arrangement and a new feeling.

Rum & Coke Sip No. 1:
Inroads of tidal questionnaires,
Sun filliping toothpick sand.
Musical clouds, complicating space glints,
Triple *assemblé* upsurge through heat,
Uncertain Destiny Clouds
Droning across harrumph of horizon.

Reconnaissance clouds, sunstreak virtuosos.
Cloud names: last name first, first name,
Middle initial, maiden name,
Real name, unspoken name, unspeakable name,
Unknown name, unknowable name,
Spouse's name, spouse's occupation,
Spouse's income, own, rent, buy, mortgage.

Operatic gusts plangent over seafroth,
Beachscape darkening to teak.
Negresco stomach crease inventory
After powdery brass Negresco sunset emotion,
Negresco clouds, Upper Lip Moisture Fear.
Wave palaver. Wave bye-bye. Star waves.
Awaiting advent of The New Gorgeousness.

Awaiting departure of The Old Hideousness:
Sol, soleil, solitude, solipsism.
Despair of escaped canary snafu: achoo.
Despair of teeth and toenail obsession concession.
Implausible clouds, tottering like milk troughs
On edge of first invention of summer.
Despair of sperm wax depletion allowance.

Favorite cloud: institutional dispenser soap pink.
Lummox resurfacing. Lummox plunging.
Point of origin, destination, arrival time,
Length of stay, citizenship, nature of business,
Male, female, birth date, hotel beauty,
Cloud enigma, *grande pensée*, most fun thing to do
In one of Earth's really great Principalities.

BLUE SKIES

for Michael Faubion

Around the corner of the sky
Some birds are making themselves
Useful. They've been especially
Flown in. Odd, to see flamingoes,

Albeit paper flamingoes
Covered with handwriting,
As louvers you peer through, there
In the lithops garden

Where the day's transparent insignias
Have bloomed: a perfect scene
For the credits to roll under
While a song indelibly sad is played,

Occluding further comment
Like a man doused in gasoline.
If I step into your clothes
With you in them, I'm no better

Than a flamingo set afire,
Or into the several hearts of that flame
An idea whose time never comes.
Yet all summer long we will wait,

Gloving the stony hands of the garden,
And on through winter, too,
Until our faces, frozen
Into passport photo parodies

Of how we look, fade and ravel
Even in the minds of unborn police.
And that kitchen gadget, the one
With a thousand household uses:

We discovered only two or three,
But the universe absorbs these regrets,
Which is why space doubles back on itself
And allows no room to step outside

To rotate it in the proper fashion
So that we may return,
Like pages in a notebook,
To the lost place of unforgiven

Edification. There *was* something unholy
About the way you bulged
That plummeted us into historical time,
Though I still remember the sky's map,

How all the countries
Touch in one color, how the same glove
Fits either hand, and how a care
As of lepidopterists maneuvering in tall grass

Reigns there, dust rapidly reclaiming
The halls. The halls of dazzling light.

ITALY

Here in Italy the buildings are the color
Of dead skin and the sky is "tragic"
And the rivers are brown and turbulent
And everybody is always stopping by
To say "*Ciao!*" and then "*Ciao!*"
We think a lot about emotion, chiefly
The emotion of love. There is much to cry about.
And after, sleep. One falls in love
So as not to fall asleep. I have just awakened
To the fact that I am not in love
And am about to fall asleep or write an opera
In which someone falls asleep and dies
Or write a letter to a friend or call somebody up
To meet me later for a drink. Maybe it's too late.
Tomorrow I will go out and buy something to make me happy.
I remember standing in the train station in Pisa
Hoping to catch the sound of an American voice
In the crowd. It's good to remember such things
When you think you haven't "lived" enough
Because you need to learn not to regret
What you've never done. Fortunately, I remember
Everything that's ever happened to me.
I remember asking a woman I didn't know
Whether or not she was the person I was looking for
And she said, "Yes, much to my regret."
That wasn't difficult to remember
Because it just happened a few minutes ago.
Other things are harder. I don't remember
Right away what I had for breakfast two weeks ago
Last Thursday or the specific date of my first
Masturbation, though I'm sure that with some effort
I could recover the lasting details. I remember

My father using a green hair tonic called "H-A,"
Which stood for "Hair Arranger." I remember the night
My father tore out a big clump of my mother's hair
In an argument. They were drunk and I came out
Of my room in my pajamas and asked them to stop.
If I said I wanted to fall apart in someone's arms
You would have to assume I was being sarcastic
And you would be right. No one has arms in which
I care to fall apart, at least not at the moment.
Tomorrow night I am going to see a play about
"A contemporary man in the process of falling apart."
I think everyone falls apart about twenty times a day.
I'm still confused about why I mentioned Italy
At the beginning of this poem, especially since
It's all a terrible lie. My students would say
It means "the poet does not know where he is;
Some catastrophe has distorted his perceptions."
I am drowsy but happy and resemble the corner
Of a big empty room. I am drunk and staring
Into the bathtub. A lot of people are standing
Around listening to music. My fingers
Smell like cigarettes. I am wondering
If there is any way to describe the pleasure
Someone derives from seeing a man's cock
Shoved up someone's ass, or how one
Can go on like this, even after having given up
Completely to nervousness, and to death.
I remember the one night I spent on a ship.
The porters woke us at dawn. We stood
At the railing to sight the blue and transparent island
Gaping through mist in the distance. For breakfast,
We ate peaches. I hated the people I was with,
But I must have been incredibly stupid. We spent the day
On the island, seesawed in the park, and waded in the sea.

ARRANGEMENT

for Richard Weinstein

Often a pattern is proposed
En route to secret destinations,
On a street clothed with rain
Curving across the sun's method
Of passing unobserved through
Naked skies, as a mirror
Hides its feelings, or a photograph
Is respected for holding no opinion.

All arrangements
Compete for the same space,
Like battered kids picking their scabs,
Yet all are more remote from the ideal
Arrangement than we
From dead companions. We do not move,
Pursued by thought, every vista
Magnetized to the vanishing point
Where parallel paths of longing
Densely gather without touching,
Leaving to each of us a solitude
Resembling God's, to consider
The ripple-effect
Of one savage exhalation, rising
Without hope or skill through the volume
We displace, always evening itself out
Like water in a uniform mask
Toward the shabby little lakefront cabins,
As we tear up the waves, seeking air.

ECHO

What are the links
That tie a mind to catastrophe?
Why do you always keep track
Of how the boundaries shift
Like starlight, each flicker a cell
Of its own deterioration?

None of us is compelled to notice it
Until the hidden agenda is revealed in a memo.
We're too wrapped up in ourselves
To believe our acts throw shadows
Or that the transcript of the time will show
We stood out against the excelsior silos
Of clouds, hand in hand Red Rover fashion,
While a strawberry blazed against our lives.
The strange result was this: because
Each mattered only to himself,
Things got done, but unrenewable resources
Sprang up like partridges,
And the song of official unrest was expressed
As solo crooning.

What I don't know about you
Could fill a book. That's why I go on
Like this, using my ignorance to argue
The existence of X as a figure in the wind's
Portrait, all the while driving a truck
Through big soundless wastes between sixteenth-notes
And where I hope one day to live.

PLUSIEURS JOURS

for Bernard Welt

This end of the world feeling
October installs in the sunlight
Breathing thinly across your shoulders
Instructs our patience. Each room
Is then a lobby or vestibule to extended
Complications which will change
Not merely the sheets and towels
But the kinetic structure of events
Themselves, initiating an assault upon
The frame's indifference to what it contains:

Green fig jam on toast, eggs with parsley
And chives, apple pie, breadsticks,
Cuban coffee and fresh cream. The season
Rehearses death in the teeth of
Unassailable doubt, grown tumultuous
Through want of summer, cold air
Cleaving to your pockets, urban air sharp
And electric blue, blue as the World Series
Or Sex or blood within the vein,
Advancing toward the past as the present

Is erased amid bright, redundant
Leaves and stars. Behold the clear region
Of Heaven: it is a bedroom in a crater
Of light the size of Montana. There are
Photographs on the mantle, friends of the
Person who lives here. They have left some

Pornography scattered on the table: three
Mechanics making love beside a forklift,
Two students making love in an empty loft,
A kid and his basketball coach

Making love in the back of a truck,
Twin sisters, a swimming instructor
And a collie making love under water.
Later, we recalled that moment, but in the
Retelling it had altered, the way one's mood
Alters what we acknowledge to be happening,
So that the impetus to memory itself
Never overcomes the inertia of the attempt
To pretend there existed a time
Before we knew this way of life

Had fixed on us beyond all dream of turning
Back to blot out the more spectacular blunders
That circumstances or mere lack of judgment
Rendered inevitable; to be issued a new
Passport, a sharkskin suit, a handshake,
Twenty dollars and a bus ticket west,
And after several days to surface from sleep
Into the fabulous sun of a new life, drenched
In a weather of clemency, everything forgotten
Or lost as if swallowed by the sea.

Yet to believe this is to be like one
Who shields his eyes with his hands
And cries, "Don't see me!" You *are* seen
And you have changed into something
Infinitely adorable since I last saw you,
Though not even a mother would have you.

Listen. The afternoon is making a few
Concluding remarks among coils of branches
That remind one of useless circuitry,
And though the language is familiar

I can't make out any words, only
A generalized sense of their import,
And the rest is confusion, Mr. Interlocutor,
You who know our questions will be answered
With bad puns, laughter, or silence
Alone and that it could be no other way,
As though ordained at the beginning of time
That I should have arrived at this
Rather than that point, that you should have
Met me here to listen a while before

Turning to step beneath a porch of pied maples
And out of our lives forever. Yet someone
Always came to take your place, and the old
Canvas was not so much obliterated
As painted over, the emergent figure
Assuming its texture and relief from previous
Versions but its color from the addition
Of new pigments (acetylene white or seaweed
Fudge, for example) and its subject—
For it represented *something*, if only

The enactment of its own processes—from the
Presiding forms of our love
Which are refreshed even as they perish.
The important things remain a little way out of
Reach, just as the road to get to them
Forks off in every direction at once

Toward the horizon's brim, its meniscus
Visible and trembling right now at the first
Admittance of the sun, though what seemed
In the beginning to be the finale

Of a not especially distinguished day
Is suddenly revealed as the start
Of possibly the last day of your life,
This providential dawn finding us no nearer
The place we were heading than the sunset
We thought we were watching. But we are
Handsome in our sweaters and could be taken
For pornographic superstars in this light,
Which is flint-gray and chill and briefer
Than sparks that fly from wounded rocks.

LIVING AND BLEEDING

The merit of the day's decline is published
In fields like hair folding over

A valley. And you take up
Some new occupation, the kind forbidden
On signs leading up to the tent
Fabricated wholly of water
And resembling an astral fog interlaced
With photographs of those freshly arrived
In heaven.

It is a summer night that ambles
Up to greet us late in spring, the spokes
Of our bikes as invisible as the momentum
Bringing us here to be mounted on the air
Like TV ghosts. We
Can see them, but they can't see us:
We're the front and back of the same page,
Unknown to each other, though identical.
There is communication,
As between rooms,

Or congruent festivals, buying beer
For friends the way toenails sketch
A new economic order in the scum
Of winter swimming pools, and I cut myself
Shaving sometimes. Then another
Twenty-four hour emergency begins.

DISAPPEARING MOUNTAINS

Silent trains surge all night
Through disappearing mountains.
Some are surprised
At having forever already arrived.

But nature horrifies and instructs,
As you see only what is missing,
Wearing your body outside your clothes.
The sound of everything

Breaking would explain perspective
If you backed away. How different
These now are: shining like spurting moss
At the core of a cube of ice,

Then angling off in speeded-up slow motion,
Though perhaps this map
Is wrong, is the shape of our breath
In the fan's mouth,

A national dream in some countries.
We stand here, offhandedly,
In this meanwhile, while the distance
Slots us into itineraries

Or makes a clean break, accurate
Yet superficial: a decay.
Or like an anxious diner glimpsed
Through restaurant windows,

Who, had he lived in a previous century,
Would now be dead, you approach
"The Cat Ferris Wheel," through revolving
Doors, neither in nor out, perpetually

Making up your mind. (Your other brain
Told you all about us, the foothills
Pledging vegetable remorse,
Floodlit, and another decent fellow arriving,

America, on the screened-in porch.)
As the aspirin to the headache,
So he to you: he cures you,
America, from whose agitated peaks

Only empty funicular cars return…
Something out of *The Crawling Eye*
Has consumed the lodge! We see you, still,
By looking away, more you

In afterthought, less us when the topic
Turns round again to you like wind
And sun that flap the bedsheets dry
And are glamour to outsiders alone,

And you know who you are, distributed
Like dust after a sneeze,
In unnumbered arrondissements, our minutes kept
Re-remembering you.

IN THE EMPIRE OF THE AIR

THE SKY

Here are blooms whose function is
To melt and disappear (they may be dead
Already) like vexed deer

At the rim of their preserve. Darts,
Perforations of frozen fire, the bottomless
Cup of coffee overturned above our heads

Insinuated into the expanse.
Its interior glaze is sometimes visible
Ledgered in water,

With horny teenaged skill accomplished,
As with each *frisson*
At the disposal of anatomy

Chunks of scenery are spirited
Under a penny. *But nothing fits
In the space provided.* The handful

Is bigger than the hand. All
You hear is the sound of new leaves
Turning over and over.

WINTER GARDEN

for Robert Dash

A permanent occasion
Knotted into the clouds: pink, then blue,
Like a baby holding its breath, or colorless

As the gush and pop of conversations
Under water. You feel handed from clasp to clasp,
A concert carried off by the applause.

Other times, half of you is torn
At the perforated line and mailed away.
You want to say, "Today, the smithereens

Must fend for themselves,"
And know the ever-skating decimal's joy,
To count on thin ice

Growing thinner by degrees, taking its own
Sweet time and taking us with it,
To navigate magnetic zones in which

Intense ecstatic figures touch, like worlds,
But don't collide, it being their devotion
To depend on you to name for each

A proper sphere. "Today, I turn to silence;
Let the language do the talking."
X the Unknown and his laughable, lovable crew,

The tumbling balconies of one-of-us-is-a-robot-
And-it's-*not*-me waves
(Spanking a beach so empty

If you weren't around to trip me
Would I really fall?) and days
When the wind is a bridge across our power

To enumerate, to dig, to plant, to hold
And to communicate the twill-and-tweed-
Covered field's coldness

Toward our game of enticing it indoors,
As if we could erect a rival gate to the departure
Whose uniform destination can't surprise,

Is blind, speaks not,
When on those white and sudden afternoons
I take your eyes, and see the sun set twice.

MASTERS OF SELF-ABUSE

You grow taller. Time stands in a hole, borrowing from sleep. Where you stand is borrowed, the hole of sleep is yours. No time passes. An evening's government grows old, passing its borrowed stance into a hole, to sleep until the new government stands taller.

I see new prisoners swoop past in borrowed limousines until, late in the evening, is the sleeping government still standing? Old times, newly gowned, resemble the tall prisoners asleep in a hole, where passing limousines govern the swooping from evening to evening.

You borrow your resemblance from a hole in the gown. Evening dilapidates, in time, into several pools. Each is stained to resemble a government limousine holding the sky prisoner: a standing pool of sleep newly dilapidating. You must have passed in a borrowed gown as the sky slept, a gown of islands governed by prisoners of the late evening, and where you stood dilapidated. Lifting their gowns for you to swoop into sight, these evening stains hold late, resembling islands of dilapidating limousines asleep in the old sky.

I wonder what dilapidating prisoners think of the infinity of stains. Each island fits its hold, but where each resemblance? I want to touch the hole, to gown its pool of imprisoned sleep in borrowed, swooping light and lift the stain out of government. A wonderful pool stains the island it touches, a dilapidated light resembling sleep. The sky is a fit government until time borrows several thoughts from the limousine pool, and each gowned prisoner swoops from sight in the sleep of an infinite evening.

You blame the government for the island's dilapidated sleep (I must have been part of that machine): an infinity of paper limousines standing in a pool of city light that fits in a hole (the sunlit evenings, the sleeping pools, vanishing into the sky) in the sky. Is this future yours, borrowed from a prisoner? (Is the tone to blame for a hole in the sun?) Or are the islands, asleep in paper gowns, stained by some resemblance to the future, holding you to blame? Will cities of the future be prisoners (the prisoners think the tone resembles paper cities out of the past, old limousines performing in their sleep) untouched by light, wondering where the islands grew still? You want to hold the evening on paper, lift the city out of its hole, sleep in a pool resembling the sun. You borrow the sky for a gown, to pass an infinity of dilapidated evenings touching the papers of a sunny future in government. Each time a new thought stains the prisoner, your sleepy resemblance papers the sky. A cool evening, asleep in some hole in the city (swooping and standing still, in the cool mechanical light that holds the city to the island and the sun in the sky's thoughts), borrowing dilapidated futures from the light. Several futures fit the growing gown, and each is a prisoner, resembling you, and sleeping late. The city, the wonder, the infinite passage of islands in vanishing limousines, holding and lifting to the sky the city and its stains: fit sights to cool the sun.

IMPRESSIONISM

What *about* the machinery
Hiding the air's reticent features

From itself? Clouds,
Scooped and redumped from and into

The tribal water-horde,
Stir up, mornings,

A dust of lurid chalks.
Then, as through the glycerin smart

Of one uncryable tear, a moron's shoelace
Forgets its bow-knot (each second's

Personal gripe ticked off like this
In the chimes' arousal) while you

In this segment are several,
The difference between you eternal.

VIRGULE

The arrow pointing three directions
Is a looser, more open form of display,
More like the subsidiary décor

A door divulges, opening upon
A continuum of hidden driveways,
Than the steep, reversible terraces

Of a zipper. Yet how often
Have I mounted a similar staircase,
Only to find myself, impatient,

On the floor below, pale
As a Pierrot on a cocktail napkin,
The level I was standing on

Now detached from the rest
Of the structure. So autumn
Exerts pressure on the fizzing,

Bright bulk of late summer,
Upends the light
To expose its corroded underbelly,

Next week and the week after
Arriving on time but ahead
Of our schedule: the ash

Of their once twice-shy contents
Sucked back into the hanging fire
That burns you at both ends.

IN BALLET, YOU ARE ALWAYS A "BOY"

In ballet, you are always a "boy,"
Growing up into unmade suits
Whose sleeves will deny
Any knowledge of you. For the day
Is wide, yet fixed, a stream
Eddying into smudge mist,
Seemingly penciled in
Beneath this sky's magnesium flash,
Though more real than grief
And what you cannot yet have remembered—
Whistled or hummed. Later,
When we have less time, we may know
What we know now in an altered light
That bleeds from below, stairs
Burning above, passing a wintry dusk
In the ordinary way,
And feel reappear in a breeze
Floating about a column
The close, the familiar moisture,
The unheeding fluidity
Of the old days and years.

SANTA

Santa is the incomplete
Embodiment of our charity. Poor Santa,
His many bodies minted
Of human waste, his voice the choir
Of his own need. I feel so empty,
By myself, whispering my lists
In Santa's spiral ear, while he lists
Slightly to one side like skeet
Propelled into the air by a device
No human hand has touched, so obsolete
Is effort when a dime skims ice.
Emit a cry for every useless thing:
Abundant padding so contrived
No one of us shall feel deprived.

IN THE EMPIRE OF THE AIR

Scourging the sea with rods
To punish it for what it has engulfed,
Or running naked with your bronzed friend
Through yellow broom sage:
You can't be sure which remedy will be
Fatal, or whether the density of the side-effects
Will prevent you from moving backwards
Across the threshold, to read
What the instructions might have said
If anyone had taken time to write them down,
So we could torture the words, make them
Confess their dirty little secret. It's tiered,
As earth is, with faults perfectly expressing
A gravitational will that we should stumble
Over them. And all the hints
Get sponged up at night. Above the land fill—
Stars, glowing zircon strands of dump truck highbeams
Lined up, liquid and radiant, past the last
Open-all-night erotica boutique
Just over the state line of the last state.
Maybe they're sparks we ignite
Rubbing each other the wrong way, fiery notes
Unwary rhapsodists pluck from the strings
Of incendiary violins. Is that what you think, too?
In truth, I prefer your mistaken identity,
The upside down one I can see at the back of my eyes
Before they flip you into focus, projecting you
Across a space at once so vast and so small
As not to excite even scientific curiosity.
But the light you throw off, out there,

Is not enough to see you by. The tapered crimps
And ridges, scraped into the wall of the well,
Could be any number of people. Try
To communicate with the dying sometime
And you'll know what I mean. Each one is perfect,
Of its kind. Also, all are alike. Not even they
Can tell you, though, where the similarities end,
Whether it will be any different
For you. All I know is that what you are
To the waxed, limpid air of freak May in December
Or to this room, piled high
With genial household archetypes,
Is a formal relationship only, as the shape
Of an airplane-shaped shrub is
To the living plant it's made of. But to me,
And all I said and did, and all the time
It took me to get here, so much I forgot
The purpose of my visit, but kept on anyway; to me,
As I hold you, and the messy edges
Of our privacy overlap and then withdraw—
Think of me as three persons, and as one,
But always who I am, ever changing
And complete, in the empire of the air
Or on the street, or with white sails
Stiff against the wind,
Whistling far out over the water.

THE LAKE EVENING

No one contradicts the view
These windows administer
On lawn or lake:

Dead lawn, dry lake,
Green and blue and golf-green,
Blue waters prodding the lake's skin,
As if a giant heart pumped within,
Needling its chart
In the sopping grass. Bare
Or furnished trees wave "Hi,"
But by the sheer force of their beauty
Become invisible, aloof
From that sort of vast variety show
Of which you get a hint
Here and there. Held in reserve,
These come to you last of all,
Are the last whose love you shall
Relinquish because you have taken
Longer to get to love them,
Or acquire control.

Dear Horrible:
    Everything that acquires reality in time comes deracinated,
like moonlight that prevents the stirring leaves to distinguish an
area set aside, its shape sovereign over the volume it announces and
protects, not similar to human lives because richer, and containing
less hardship.

Our attention whets smooth
The lake's plumed surface. The night
Is brief, life is briefer, nothing else
Dares to move. We think
The business of the day'll
Take care of us. Beyond those bluffs,
Where we vanish,
As at the summit of a rope,
Is only wondering.

AFTERWORD

by Douglas Crase

The appearance in print of the selected poems of Donald Britton is an affront to cynicism and a triumph over fate. When Donald died, in 1994, it was sadly reasonable to assume that the influence of his poetry would be confined to the few who had preserved a copy of his single book, the slender, deceptively titled *Italy*, published thirteen years earlier. As the few became fewer it seemed all but certain the audience for his poems would disappear. Donald never taught, so there were no students to mature into positions of critical authority. There was no keeper of the flame to incite publication, no posthumous foundation to subsidize it, not even a martyrology in place to demand it out of sentiment. The survival of his work would have to come about, instead, as a pure instance of "go little booke"—an instance that must now warm the heart of anyone who has ever believed in poetry. It was the poems in *Italy* themselves, free of professional standing or obligation, that inspired the successive affections of two remarkable editors and the confident publisher of the present selection. Donald, who despite his brilliance was a modest and self-effacing person, would be surprised.

I met Donald on New Year's Eve, 1978, at a crowded party hosted by Michael Lally in his loft on Duane Street in the section of Manhattan since called Tribeca. The first thing one noticed about Donald, having registered already at a distance that he was blond ("dirt blond," he once corrected me), was the beauty of his high forehead. His eyes were blue, or 298U in the Pantome matching system (he informed me of that, as well), familiar today as the color of the Twitter logo and known sometimes as Twitter blue. But the arresting feature was the forehead, a placid expanse that seemed the emblem of intellect and imparted to his face an overall composure that persisted through even the most animated moments. The effect could be misleading. It defeated the initial efforts of painter Larry Stanton, whose portraits of Donald's friends Brad Gooch, Tim Dlugos, and Dennis Cooper are eerily ideal to anyone who knew them, but whose attempted likeness of Donald, as part of a triple portrait with Tim and Dennis, resembles the demented hitchhiker of your worst nightmare. The forehead has distorted the face, and each fix Larry applied—he even changed the haircut—made the image less satisfactory. A subsequent effort, the double portrait of a *noir* Dennis and beatific Donald, was dramatically more successful. Larry was so pleased he kept this second painting a secret until its exhibition at a private gallery in the East Village, where Donald would see it for the first time the night of the opening.

Donald came to New York from Washington, D.C., following the example of Tim, who likewise had followed a trail blazed earlier by Michael Lally. In Washington, Michael was a founder of the Mass Transit reading series that gave Tim and other now prominent poets their early audience. By the time Donald lived in Washington, Mass Transit had been replaced by an equally influential series sponsored by Doug Lang at Folio Books. Here Donald found his own early audience. In those years, whether in Washington or New York, one's circle of poet friends was fluid, social, and embraced a heady mix of Language-centered writers and latter-day disciples of the New York School. You could meet Bruce Andrews at a party and not fear you had compromised his aesthetic. Donald thus took for granted that there was more than one way to articulate the times, and he respected any poetics that would approach the task seriously. That he himself approached it seriously is apparent from his work of this period: "*La plus belle plage*," with its careening nouns that nonetheless verge on narrative, or "Notes on the Articulation of Time," with its observation that "We need / these narratives, we want them." One might conclude he had therefore chosen sides, as Kenward Elmslie implied in a blurb for *Italy* claiming Donald as a "super-Ashbery-of-the-Sunbelt." But if that was humorous then, it is misleading today. The early "Serenade" (which I hadn't seen until Philip Clark obtained it from Donald's correspondence with a friend) is a reminder of a moment in our poetry when it was possible to conceive of uniting Eliot and Hart Crane, under the tutelage of Mallarmé and perhaps the wary eye of Pound, and so make an end run around

Ashbery altogether. If Donald came out sometimes at the place Ashbery was to occupy a week later, well, this made the result no less worthy and gave him an insight, meanwhile, into the reproducible strategies of genius.

Taking up residence in New York put Donald in contact with a wider circle of writers and artists, many of whom still basked in the glow generated by Ashbery and the other poets known originally as the New York School. Dennis Cooper, who was to live in the city from 1983 to 1985, described in a later interview the excitement of being introduced to that circle by his friends. "I'd go to a party with Tim and Donald and Brad," remarked Dennis, "and there would be slightly older writers like Joe Brainard and Kenward Elmslie and Ron Padgett, and then the established greats like Ashbery and Schuyler and Edwin Denby, and nonpoets too, like Donald Barthelme and Alex Katz and Roy Lichtenstein and just an incredibly multigenerational group of artists, gay and straight, who felt some kind of aesthetic and personal unity." That unity was more than notional. The figures named (all male, but there were women at those gatherings, too) shared for the most part a faith in chance and daily experience, a faith that whatever came in through the open window would be redemptive and nourishing, or else no worse than a disappointment, which would be nourishing as well. Tim and Eileen Myles adapted this faith to liberating effect; Eileen tagged it accurately as an aesthetic of "exalted mundanity." But Donald had his doubts. He had acquired a good dose of skepticism from his Language-oriented colleagues in D.C., internalized the skepticism of Shakespeare while performing the plays at the University of Texas, and probably learned, long before, the survival skepticism of the wise child who grows up in a provincial town. Tim occasionally wrote parodies of his poet friends and the one he dedicated to Donald, "Qum," already captured Donald's growing unease with the poetics of exalted mundanity and Language both: "Wanting people to desire us / we (meaning you and I) wear a bright veil / of language (meaning words) before which pale / the mundane elements of waking life."

Considering the dual spell of spectacle and diminishment that had begun to fasten its grip on New York and the rest of the country, a degree of unease was justified. The proposition that chance would always be nourishing appeared less obvious, for instance, as social and economic prospects were being hollowed out. Meanwhile, there was the spectacle. With momentous timing, Donald's first year in the city had turned out to be the year the band Blondie released their chart-topping single "Heart of Glass." A New Wave lyric aloft on a disco sound, "Heart of Glass" was regarded by some as a sellout and by others as a vindication of downtown. Donald and his friends favored the downtown clubs, but anywhere one went—bars, restaurants, the drugstore—this was the song most played. Viewed today the video may look quaint, but Debbie Harry never will, and the pulsing 24-track mix as one awaits her perfect lip-sync of the words "pain in the ass" should demonstrate what an overwhelming experience the club scene was. Donald's preferred moment in the lyrics, by the way, was "mucho mistrust." It was a diagnostic delight on his part even then; because disco, whether maligned or meant for the young and free, offered a taste of spectacles to come whose design was to stun the individual spirit, not augment it. Personal history might be "annihilated, ground / Into a very fine talc," to use Donald's words from the poem he titled, inevitably it seems, "Heart of Glass." Since his poems possess, as he did, a kind of intimate reserve, they are likely to be read as if they lived on literary allusion alone, without reference to politics or popular culture. But the distant allusion to Rimbaud in Donald's "Heart of Glass" (especially the "*Parade*"-like twist at the ending), and a possible allusion to the Herzog film of the same title, only lend depth to the poem as the meditation on spectacle it is. To read it with the clubs in mind is to be present in the strobe lights as inside a Venetian bead, on the dance floor as the little threshing floor of earth, and better prepared for the indulgent but unsettling ending in which the awed hero "elated at the portrayal of things beyond his ken / Shouldered his people's glorious future." In a manner consistent with the best work of his maturity, Donald's "Heart of Glass" has the uncanny effect of having been our history, written ahead of time.

Donald never discussed at length, at least not with me, the theory behind his poems. For an explicit quotation one has to rely on his published statement in *Ecstatic Occasions, Expedient Forms*. But with "Heart of Glass" in evidence, I can safely testify that he intended his poetry to enable, rather than disable language, in the belief that poetry so energized was the ideal vehicle to move us beyond "mucho mistrust" to the usable illusion of discourse. The alternative idea that he might divest himself of language and repossess it once it was purged of injustice would have seemed, as the years went by, quixotic if not credulous. How long did one have to wait? The blunt truth was that you articulate the narrative of your time or someone of another party will articulate it for you, and you don't have all day. One of Donald's endearing habits in this regard was to mark the temporal narrative of our lives by planning his own birthday celebrations. For his thirty-first birthday he arranged dinner at a Tex-Mex restaurant from which we could walk afterward to the piano bar Marie's Crisis, where Tim drove us nuts belting out from memory the show tunes he all too clearly loved to sing. For his thirty-third birthday he picked a trendier restaurant, this time more Tex than Mex, on West 55th Street. Frank and I (Frank Polach, my lover and once the law allowed, husband) discovered on arrival that we had to ring the buzzer as if for a private club. Being several years older than Donald and his other friends, we felt fortunate to be included. Upstairs we found Brad and the director Howard Brookner, the most electrically beautiful couple we knew; Chris Cox, writer and photographer, who when we first met him was the lover of Edmund White; Dennis and Rob Dickerson, whose upturned face appears in a photo by Chris on the cover of Dennis's novella *Safe*; and Donald and David Cobb Craig, who had been Donald's partner for about a year and would remain so to the end. Tim wasn't there. He had dated David first and at the time of this party regarded Donald as a treacherous thief.

A knowing reader may suspect today that Donald's plan to let language follow its own initiative was equivalent to the supposedly hopeless search for a safe passage between "parataxis" and "hypotaxis," that is to say, between the Scylla of nothing but upright nouns and the Charybdis of seductive syntax. I remember it instead as an instinctive behavior that permitted him to proceed as if the dilemma didn't exist, as it probably doesn't. Donald intended his poetry to be impersonal, or "non-personalized," as he put it; but he expected it to issue all the same from personal encounters with friends and life, affairs and betrayals, necessities and emergencies. That was the point of the birthday dinners, my retelling and his planning them in the first place. There wasn't much talk of prosody at those events. Criticism was communicated by an eye roll, groan, laughter, or shared enthusiasm. And yet it was Donald who insisted with enthusiasm that we read, and better yet get to know, Marjorie Welish; he once planned her birthday dinner, too. Their subsequent friendship, given Marjorie's observed rigor and his apparent romance, warrants a second look at both. And it was Donald who insisted we attend a lecture at Cooper Union in which Tim analyzed meticulously the art of Larry Stanton, Joe Brainard, Bill Sullivan, and Trevor Winkfield (who did the black-and-white cover art for *Italy*). By then Donald had his heart set on acquiring a Winkfield of his own and would be thrilled, years later, when he was able to buy *Landscape with Interior* direct from Trevor's studio. The abstractions he took from such personal encounter were compressed deep in Donald's poems: an homage to Brainard's *I Remember* hidden midway in "Italy," a bow to Marjorie's recursive disciplines in "Masters of Self-Abuse," a recovery of Bernard Welt's prose outcrops in "The Lake Evening." There was even a gentle dig at my own preoccupations in "Disappearing Mountains." By no means, however, was there indiscriminate approval. Because he had asked me once if he shouldn't "do more for his career," I suggested we make a raid on the 92nd Street Y, the primary venue in New York at that time for poets of grandeur. I must have thought any event would do. The reader that night was Robert Penn Warren, which was grand indeed, and Donald's dismay as we sat trapped in the auditorium through the interminable reading was palpable. Having made it to the end, we decided to brave the reception, hypocrites on the make. But Donald was soon ready to flee. "Awful," he told me. "Dismal." Those were his words. He never asked what to "do for his career" again.

The language Donald achieved in his poems was frequently so ravishing that one could virtually feel the pleasure of his mind as it coursed over the emerging syntax, a kind of pleasure he identified indelibly in "Winter Garden" as "the ever-skating decimal's joy." Some theorists have complained, of course, that a poetry of obliging syntax tends inescapably to nostalgia for fantasies that could never exist. A happy decimal must be a case in point. Donald himself was sympathetic to the charge, which is why he acknowledged in his statement for *Ecstatic Occasions* that he might be accused of a naïve belief in the language of flowers and voiceless things, *le langage des fleurs et des choses muettes.* (It's Baudelaire, from "Élévation," and Donald did know French.) Still, it is peculiar that poets of all people should apologize for an attempt to express things inexpressible, or speak for things that cannot speak. I suppose an opinion in this regard depends on where one locates the working surface of a poem. If one assumes the surface is coterminous with the visible page, then it's only natural to be interested in the physical look of words alone. If you assume the working surface of poetry is time, then it's equally natural to be interested in the invisible, voiceless precincts beyond the page. Such a distinction accounts for the sense of scale—we might call it the intimate vast—which Donald embraced in even his shortest poems. It will account, too, for the apparent prescience in his work, as in the hauntingly titled "In the Empire of the Air," written after he had met and fallen in love with David. Suddenly he seemed to anticipate the dissolution of his body and its dispersal from the art he would leave behind. Perhaps he feared already that he had the virus. Who didn't? He found his title in a sixteenth-century French poem translated into English as "The Amorous Zodiac." Witty but sexless, as witty art tends to be, "The Amorous Zodiac" conveys the poet's regret that he can't stay forever in contemplation of his love, but must be dissolved by nature into "the empire of the air," the water, or the earth. Donald's poem was certainly not sexless. Owing to its erotic charge one is driven to think of the human body, blond with a high forehead but since dispersed, that conceived and wrote it. Think of me, Donald wrote, "in the empire of the air / Or on the street, or with white sails / Stiff against the wind / Whistling far out over the water."

We first heard the reports of a mysterious illness among gay men in May 1981, only two months after *Italy* had appeared, but the first friend Donald or I knew to actually die was Larry Stanton, the painter, in 1984. After that, one lived with the certain apprehension that the friends who defined your life might suddenly wither, suffer, and disappear. The critic David Kalstone, a source of wisdom and encouragement to many of us, was hospitalized the next year and died at home on West 22nd Street in 1986. Tim tested positive in 1987 and Donald the month after he moved to Los Angeles in 1988. Howard Brookner, who stopped taking the debilitating drug AZT so he could complete his first feature-length film, *Bloodhounds of Broadway* (it stars Madonna), was moved into an apartment in Frank's and my building and died there in 1989. Tim and Chris Cox died in 1990; Joe Brainard, then Donald, in 1994. We say "died," but of course they were killed, by a threat they never could have foreseen. It's true that Donald didn't write much after the march of death began, although the heart-trapping "*Zona Temperata*" is sufficient by itself to stand for the suspended aspirations of his final years. He would not have dramatized his situation and, as one can tell from his poems, didn't consider the individual case to be that interesting. More to the point was the brute fact that his living tradition had been traumatized and traumatically taken away. The infrastructure he relied on for a roll of the eyes or hoot of approval was simply in ruins. Because that infrastructure is by its nature private, even secret, I can describe Donald's situation only through an example of my own. One day Howard called unexpectedly (he was so glamorous I was shocked he knew my name) to announce with wicked delight that he hadn't read my book but Brad had taken it to the bathroom, which meant it must be important, and "Congratulations, dear." It was the funniest, finest accolade one could receive. I am sure Donald knew similar moments of surprise support, and I hope some of them came from me. But when that spontaneous network of trust is gone, you are not so much redefined as returned to a state of undefined entropy, such as you endured as a child. There is no way to repeat the young adulthood during which poets, like others, make their lifelong friends. People who survived, or were never even in danger, shouldn't crow about the superior longevity of their careers.

Donald's posthumous success in inspiring the publication of his selected poems, coupled with the undeniable failure in worldly terms of his career, is occasion to wonder if the career is ever the same as poetry itself. From time to time a critic will observe that Hart Crane's suicide, for example, or Joe Brainard's decision to stop making art, may be regarded as proof the artist realized what his admirers don't, that the work was a failure and the career could not be sustained. The critic doesn't quite dare to draw the same conclusion from the abjuration of Rimbaud or the suicide of Sylvia Plath, which reveals of course that the logic in the first case was as opportunistic as it is preposterous. Someday a critic will do us the service of disentangling poetry from the standard map of a professional career. The map is a convenience to committees but meaningless to the future reader— the twelve-year-old boy or girl in San Angelo—the very reader poets must hope to have. What is useful to that boy or girl is sometimes no more than a phrase, perhaps a book or poem, amounting to a style of mind in which to escape or dwell. I recognized such a style of mind in Donald Britton and it made us friends. The first time I heard him read his work in public was at the Ear Inn in New York, the afternoon of March 7, 1981. Blond as ever, he was in that environment an apparition of nervous grace. I can't say he connected with the audience; he certainly didn't flatter it. He conveyed, perhaps too clearly for the occasion, his sense of an audience beyond the room. One got the feeling he expected to reach across time and elicit a response composed of the same respect for intellect and desire that we had there, in the Ear Inn, that Saturday afternoon. Donald's poems were not lessons or anecdotes. They are invitations to the unending contemplation of ourselves, and things beyond us, that makes the human species a window on creation.

BIBLIOGRAPHICAL NOTES

Donald Britton kept no formal record of his publications. The following alphabetical list of titles, which I have pieced together from the acknowledgments in *Italy* and numerous other sources, is therefore undoubtedly incomplete. It is offered here for those who may wish to envision the constellation of small press magazines and anthologies where Britton's work has appeared. I have chosen to include the titles of poems that Reginald and I did not select for *In the Empire of the Air*, along with prose writings, in order that anyone who wishes to read additional work by Donald Britton may do so.

Annual Survey of American Poetry (1985): "In the Empire of the Air"

Art issues No. 2 (February 1989): "German Expressionism, 1915-1925" (review)

Art issues No. 4 (May 1989): "The Dark Side of Disneyland (Part I)" (essay)

Art issues No. 5 (Summer 1989): "The Dark Side of Disneyland (Part II)" (essay)

Art issues No. 6 (September/October 1989): "Peter Shelton" (review)

Art issues No. 7 (November 1989): "The Dada and Surrealist Word-Image" (review)

Art issues No. 11 (May 1990): "Lari Pittman" (cover essay)

Art issues No. 15 (December 1990/January 1991): "Mike Kelley" (review)

Barney No. 1 (1981): "In Ballet, You Are Always a "Boy""

Christopher Street 3, No. 5 (December 1978): "*La Plus Belle Plage.*"

Coming Attractions: An Anthology of American Poets in Their Twenties (Los Angeles: Little Caesar Press, 1980), ed. Dennis Cooper: "Heart of Glass"; "*Non Piangere, Donald!*"; "Notes on the Articulation of Time"; "September Night"; "We Loved the Inexact"

Dog City No. 1 (1977): "Caspar David Friedrich is Sad"; "Ferdinand de Saussure is Sad"; "Notes on the Articulation of Time"

Dog City No. 2 (1980): "Blue Skies"

Ecstatic Occasions, Expedient Forms: 65 Leading Contemporary Poets Select and Comment on Their Poems (New York: Macmillan, 1987), ed. David Lehman: "Winter Garden"

Epoch XXXIII, No. 1 (Fall/Winter 1983): "Winter Garden"

Forehead 2 (1990): "Santa"

Hanging Loose 104 (Spring 2014): "A Real Life"

Là-bas No. 11 (March/April 1978): "We Loved the Inexact"; "Signs"; "*La Plus Belle Plage*"; "*Non Piangere, Donald!*"; "The Certain Body."

Little Caesar No. 10 (1980): "White Space"

Little Caesar No. 11 (1980): "Italy"

Lucille Poetry Journal No. 5 (Spring 1975): "Hart Crane Saved from Drowning (Isle of Pines, 1926)"; "A Man Feeding the Birds," "An Amorous Day," "Three Sketches"; "Large Winter Scene"

Lucille Poetry Journal No. 7 (Spring 1976): "My Mother's Afternoon Nap"; "All Saints' Eve"; "Three Songs"

Mothers of Mud 1, No. 4 (March 1982): "The Sky"; "Impressionism"

Mythomania: Fantasies, Fables, and Sheer Lies in Contemporary American Popular Art (Los Angeles: Art issues. Press, 1996) by Bernard Welt: "The Dark Side of Disneyland" (essay)

Oink! 17 (1983): "Masters of Self-Abuse"

Paris Review 27, No. 97 (Fall 1985): "In the Empire of the Air"; "Virgule"

The Paris Review Anthology (New York: Norton, 1990), ed. George Plimpton: "Virgule"

Persistent Voices: Poetry by Writers Lost to AIDS (New York: Alyson, 2009), eds. Philip Clark and David Groff: "Sonnet"; "Hart Crane Saved from Drowning (Isle of Pines, 1926)"; "*Zona Temperata*"; "Notes on the Articulation of Time"

Poetry in Motion No. 10 (Winter 1979): "Heart of Glass"

Poetry in Motion No. 11 (Spring 1980): "September Night"; "Spontaneous Bruises"

Some Other Magazine No. 5 (Summer 1981): "The Lake Evening"

The Son of the Male Muse: New Gay Poetry (Trumansburg: The Crossing Press, 1983), ed. Ian Young: "History"; "Sonnet" (both from "Four Poems")

Spazio Umano / Human Space No. 2 (April-June 1988): "Virgule"; "The Sky" (translations by Jonathan Galassi)

Sun and Moon No. 8 (Fall 1979): "Capital Life"; "*Plusieurs Jours*"

The Washington Review of the Arts 3, No. 4 (December/January 1977-1978): "Elevators I"; "Elevators II"

The Washington Review of the Arts 5, No. 3 (October/November 1979): *Je Suis Ein Americano* by Tim Dlugos (review)

BIOGRAPHICAL NOTES

Raised in San Angelo, Texas, DONALD BRITTON earned a Ph.D. at American University, where he wrote his dissertation about Hart Crane, before moving to New York City in 1979. Britton's sole volume of poetry, *Italy*, was published by Little Caesar Press in 1981. Further poems and essays appeared in various publications until his death in Los Angeles, in July 1994, at age 43.

REGINALD SHEPHERD was a prolific poet, essayist, and editor. His ten books include the poetry collections *Wrong, Fata Morgana,* and *Red Clay Weather,* the essay collections *Orpheus in the Bronx* and *A Martian Muse,* and the anthologies *The Iowa Anthology of New American Poetries* and *Lyric Postmodernisms.*

PHILIP CLARK is co-editor of the anthology *Persistent Voices: Poetry by Writers Lost to AIDS.* He lives near Washington, D.C., where he researches and writes about gay history and literature.

DOUGLAS CRASE is a former MacArthur Fellow and author of the poetry collection *The Revisionist.*

NIGHTBOAT BOOKS

Nightboat Books, a nonprofit organization, seeks to develop audiences for writers whose work resists convention and transcends boundaries. We publish books rich with poignancy, intelligence, and risk. Please visit our website, www.nightboat.org, to learn about our titles and how you can support our future publications.

The following individuals have supported the publication of this book. We thank them for their generosity and commitment to the mission of Nightboat Books:

Elizabeth Motika
Benjamin Taylor

In addition, this book has been made possible, in part, by grants from The Fund for Poetry, The National Endowment for the Arts, and The New York State Council on the Arts Literature Program.